Our Bodies

Our Skin

Charlotte Guillain

Heinemann Library
Chicago, Illinois

www.heinemannraintree.com
Visit our website to find out
more information about
Heinemann-Raintree books.

To order:

☎ Phone 888-454-2279
⌨ Visit www.heinemannraintree.com
to browse our catalog and order online.

Editorial: Rebecca Rissman, Laura Knowles, Nancy Dickmann,
and Sian Smith
Picture research: Ruth Blair and Mica Brancic
Designed by Joanna Hinton-Malivoire
Original Illustrations © Capstone Global Library Ltd. 2010
Illustrated by Tony Wilson
Printed and bound by Leo Paper Group

14 13 12 11 10
10 9 8 7 6 5 4 3 2 1

Library of Congress Cataloging-in-Publication Data
Guillain, Charlotte.
 Our skin / Charlotte Guillain.
   p. cm. -- (Our bodies)
 Includes bibliographical references and index.
 ISBN 978-1-4329-3597-9 (hc) -- ISBN 978-1-4329-3606-8 (pb)
1. Skin--Juvenile literature. I. Title.
 QP88.5.G85 2010
 612.7'9--dc22
                    2009022301

Acknowledgments
The author and publisher are grateful to the following for
permission to reproduce copyright material:
Corbis pp.**10**, **23** (© Randy Faris), **13**, **23** (© Dylan Ellis), **19** (© Ronnie
Kaufman); Photolibrary pp.**15**, **16**, **4** (© Image Source), **8** (© Fancy),
12 (© Digital Vision), **14** (© Michael Weber/Imagebroker.net); **17** (©
Florence Delva/Self-Photos Agency), **20** (© Fresh Food Images), **21** (©
Radius Images), **22** (© Image Source); Science Photo Library pp.**9** (©
Mauro Fermariello), **11**, **23** (© Edward Kinsman), **18** (© Ian Boddy);
Shutterstock pp.**5** (© Andreas Gradin), **7** (© Orla).

Front cover photograph of two boys reproduced with permission of
Corbis (© Flynn Larsen). Back cover photograph reproduced with
permission of Shutterstock (© Orla).

Every effort has been made to contact copyright holders of any
material reproduced in this book. Any omissions will be rectified in
subsequent printings if notice is given to the publisher.

Contents

Body Parts

Our bodies have many parts.

head

skin

hand

leg

Our bodies have parts on
the outside.

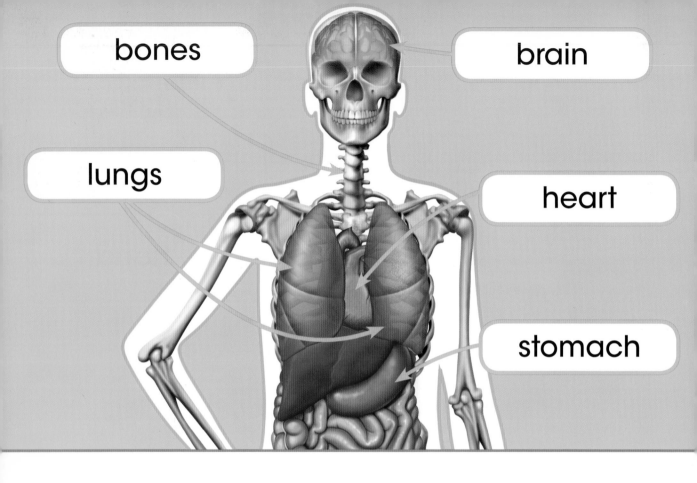

bones

brain

lungs

heart

stomach

Our bodies have parts on the inside.

skin

Your skin is on the outside of
your body.

Your Skin

You can see your skin.

Your skin is all over your body.

What Does Skin Do?

Your skin keeps the inside of your body safe.

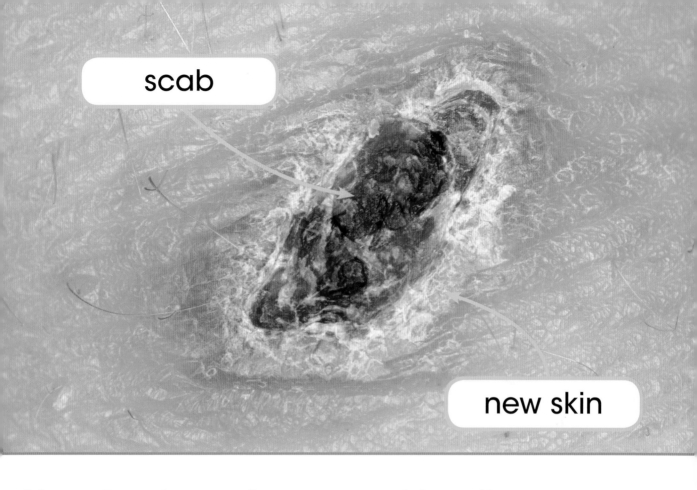

scab

new skin

Your body makes new skin all
the time.

Your skin stops you from getting too hot or too cold.

sweat

Your skin makes sweat to cool you down.

You can feel with your skin.

You can feel hot or cold things.

What Is Skin Like?

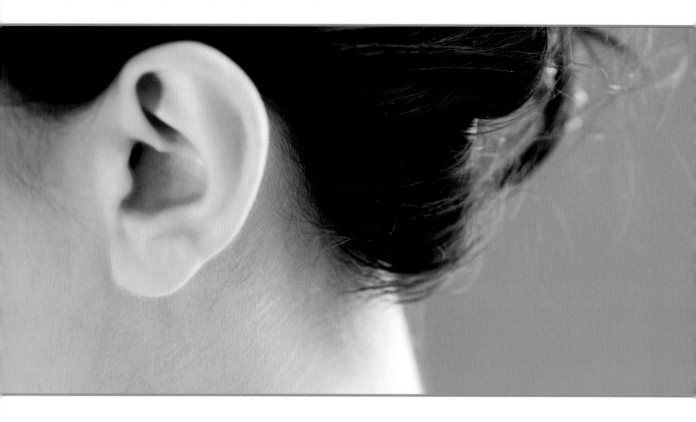

Most of your skin is soft.

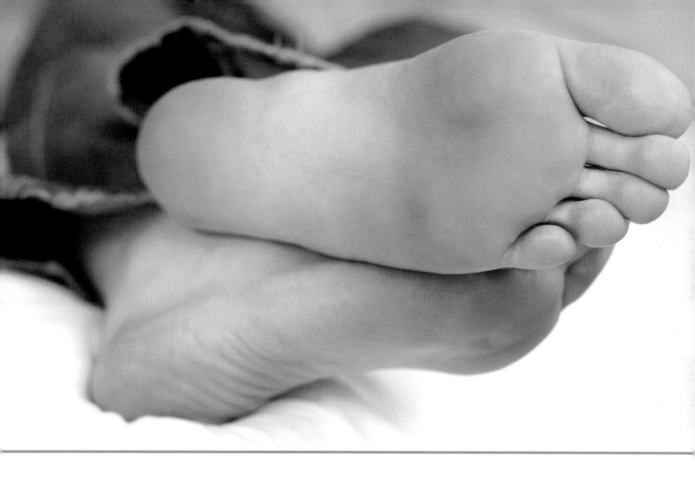

Some of your skin is harder.

Skin can be different colors.

Skin can be hairy or smooth.

Staying Healthy

You can eat healthy food to help your skin.

You can keep out of the sun to help your skin.

Quiz

Where on your body is your skin?

Answer on page 24

Picture Glossary

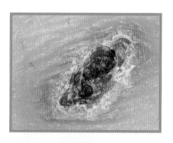

scab something your body makes to cover up a cut on your skin. New skin starts to grow under the scab.

skin waterproof covering on the outside of our bodies

sweat salty water our bodies make to cool us down

Index

Answer to quiz on page 22: Your skin is all over your body.

Notes to parents and teachers
Before reading
Ask the children to name the parts of their body they can see on the outside. Then ask them what parts of their body are inside. Make a list of them together and see if the children know what each body part does, for example, stomachs break down food. Discuss where their skin is and ask if anyone knows what skin is for.

After reading
- Ask the children to make posters telling other children how to protect their skin in the sun. They should think about what clothes to wear, sunhats, sun block, and the best times of day to play outside.
- Give children magazines and newspapers and ask them to find pictures of people with different skin (different colors, wrinkled, smooth, hairy, etc.). Then have children cut out these photos and glue them onto a piece of paper to make a collage.